Building with Shapes

by Rebecca Weber

Content Adviser: Jeffrey Hartnett, M.Arch.,
Assistant Professor, School of Architecture,
University of Nevada, Las Vegas

Reading Adviser: Rosemary G. Palmer, Ph.D.,
Department of Literacy, College of Education,
Boise State University

Spyglass
BOOKS

COMPASS POINT BOOKS

Minneapolis, Minnesota

Compass Point Books
3109 West 50th Street, #115
Minneapolis, MN 55410

Visit Compass Point Books on the Internet at *www.compasspointbooks.com*
or e-mail your request to *custserv@compasspointbooks.com*

Photographs ©: Dan Trypak/The Image Finders, cover; Patti McConville/Dembinsky Photo Associates, 4; Stock Montage, 5, 9; James P. Rowan, 6, 17; Tom Till, 7, 15; John Foxx/ImageState, 8; Alan Schein Photography/Corbis, 10; John Heseltine/Corbis, 11; Bachmann/The Image Finders, 12; Corbis, 13; John Elk III, 14; John Madere/Corbis, 16; Alex Bartel/The Image Finders, 18, 19; Angelo Hornak/Corbis, 20; Michael St. Maur Sheil/Corbis, 21.

Creative Director: Terri Foley
Managing Editor: Catherine Neitge
Editor: Jennifer VanVoorst
Photo Researcher: Svetlana Zhurkina
Designer: Les Tranby
Educational Consultant: Diane Smolinski

Library of Congress Cataloging-in-Publication Data
Weber, Rebecca.
  Building shapes / by Rebecca Weber.
    v. cm. — (Spyglass books)
  Includes bibliographical references and index.
  Contents: What shapes do you see?—Cubes—Domes—Ovals—
  Cylinders—Pyramids—Cones—Arches—Other great shapes.
  ISBN 0-7565-0655-7 (hardcover)
  1. Architecture—Composition, proportion, etc.—Juvenile literature.
  2. Form (Aesthetics)—Juvenile literature. [1. Architecture. 2. Shape.]
  I. Title. II. Series.
  NA2760.W38 2004
  720'.1—dc22   2003024098

Contents

NOTE: Glossary words are in *bold* the first time they appear.

What Shapes Do You See?

Have you ever looked closely at your home or school? Look around you. Every building in the world is made of shapes!

The ancient *Romans* were great builders. They created types of buildings we still see today.

Cubes

Many buildings are shaped like cubes. Cubes look like blocks.

Skyscrapers often look like many cubes stacked next to each other and on top of one another.

More than 1,000 years ago, some Native Americans built towns of cube-shaped rooms stacked up to four stories high.

Domes

Many buildings have domes. Domes are roofs shaped like half a ball. The United States Capitol has a domed roof.

dome

dome

The ancient Romans built
this domed-roof building
called the Pantheon. It is
still standing today.

Ovals

Some buildings have an oval shape. An oval looks like a circle that has been stretched at the top and bottom.

Many sports *stadiums* are ovals.

The Romans also built oval stadiums. They built the Colosseum in the year 80.

Cylinders

Some buildings are shaped like a cylinder. A cylinder is long and thin with curved sides like a tube. Some of the world's tallest buildings look like cylinders.

The Leaning Tower of Pisa is a famous building shaped like a cylinder.

13

Pyramids

Some buildings are pyramids. Pyramids have a square bottom and four sides shaped like triangles. The triangles come to a point on top.

A museum in Paris, France, has a glass pyramid entrance.

The Louvre Museum

14

The pyramids of Egypt
are about 4,500 years old.
Many are still standing.

Cones

Some buildings have a cone shape. Cones are circular at one end and pointed at the other.

An airport in Denver, Colorado, has a roof made of giant white cones.

Some Native Americans made *tepees* shaped like cones.

Arches

An ***arch*** is a common building shape first used by the Romans. Many buildings and bridges have arches.

keystone

An arch is made with a special stone called a keystone. The keystone is placed at the top of the curve of the arch. It holds the arch in place.

Other Great Shapes

Some buildings have very different shapes. A museum in New York City is built in the shape of a giant *spiral.*

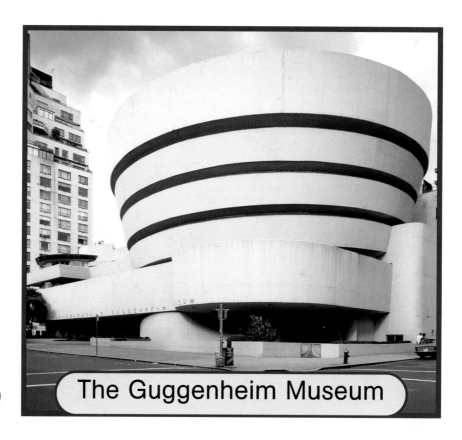

The Guggenheim Museum

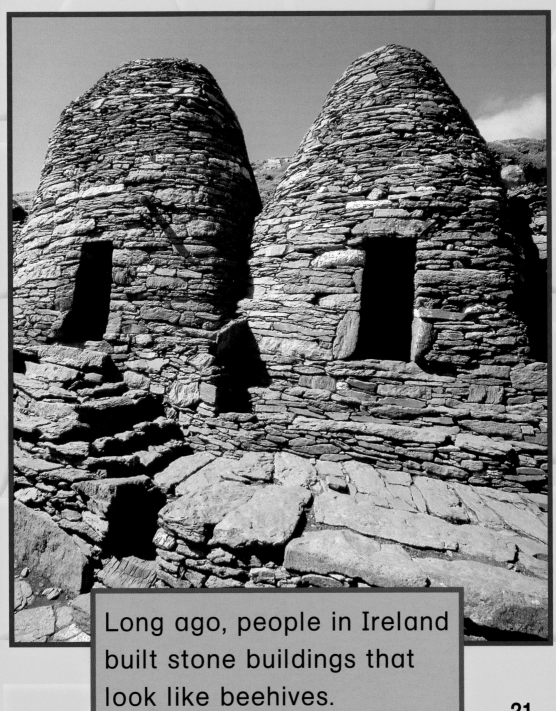

Long ago, people in Ireland
built stone buildings that
look like beehives.

21

Glossary

arch–a curved structure that often helps
    support buildings and bridges

Romans–people who lived in ancient Rome

skyscrapers–very tall buildings

spiral–a pattern that winds around in circles

stadiums–large buildings where sports
    events or concerts are held

tepees–cone-shaped tents usually made
    from animal skins

Learn More

Books

Canizares, Susan, and Samantha Berger. *Building Shapes.* New York: Scholastic, 1999.

Richards, Jon. *Shapes and Structures.* Brookfield, Conn.: Copper Beech Books, 2000.

On the Web

For more information on *Building with Shapes,* use FactHound to track down Web sites related to this book.

1. Go to *www.facthound.com*
2. Type in a search word related to this book or this book ID: 0756506557.
3. Click on the *Fetch It* button.

Your trusty FactHound will fetch the best Web sites for you!

Index

GR: J
Word Count: 225

From Rebecca Weber

Whenever I travel to a new place, I enjoy learning about people and their daily lives. I hope this book opens up a little bit of the world for you!